To Alan

I offer you my sincerest thanks for all your creative assistance and friendly encouragement from "behind the magic curtain". May the spirit of wisdom and charming affection enfold you all the days of your life, both in this world and beyond Her azure shores.

Peace & blessings,

Craig

October, 2011

# Taking Tea in the Black Rose

# Taking Tea in the Black Rose

*Singing Through the Shadows*
*Until We're Dancing in the Light*

Craig A. Combs

BALBOA.
PRESS
A DIVISION OF HAY HOUSE

*Balboa Press books may be ordered through booksellers or by contacting:*

*Balboa Press*
*A Division of Hay House*
*1663 Liberty Drive*
*Bloomington, IN 47403*
*www.balboapress.com*
*1-(877) 407-4847*



*ISBN: 978-1-4525-3841-9 (sc)*
*ISBN: 978-1-4525-3842-6 (hc)*
*ISBN: 978-1-4525-3843-3 (e)*

*Library of Congress Control Number: 2011914856*

*Printed in the United States of America*

*Balboa Press rev. date: 09/20/2011*

# CONTENTS

*To my mom for her enduring love and for never letting me give up hope; to my family and friends for continually reassuring me I have all it takes to bring this project to fruition; to everyone who shares their love freely, with a courageous spirit and an adventurous heart; and to those who still dare to take the chances life so graciously offers, come what may—I hope your own journey towards creative self-realization brings you great loves and greater chances for peace, within you as well as without. I thank each of you for sharing your sorrows and joys with me, and for now accepting this treasure from my heart I dedicate to you.*

"For those of you who run from tears
life was over before it began
Broken are the hours that build up the years
when sorrowless love hides under your nose
So I take my tea like a mystery
in the solitude of the Black Rose"

# PREFACE

Since I was a small boy growing up in rural America, I have always imagined one day traveling into outer space, exploring new planets and life forms in faraway galaxies, and boldly navigating the vast oceans of infinity. With just a few close friends and family members to share this adventure with me, I envisioned setting out from Planet Earth with only the clothes I had on my back and whatever my backpack could carry, with the hope of discovering a new world all of us could be proud of, based simply on the most timeless of principles—compassion, honesty, service, and right action.

However, following the previous centuries of society's advancement and modernization—as well as man's ridiculous race towards global superiority—many of us seem to have lost our resonance, or kinship, with these core values; choosing instead the path that disregards these ideals in favor of the selfish aims of the individual and his immediate sphere of interest, while laying waste to the general harmony and well-being of the collective (and our planetary home) along the way. Furthermore, as we cling blindly to these narrow and small-minded aspirations, we are moreover compounding the separation and division between our physical (outer) and spiritual (inner) selves, thereby further dividing each man against his brother and prolonging the inevitable return to his wholly integrated self and a healthy devotion to life's loftier and more pleasurable pursuits.

So, as we set out into the world as young adults, as I did in 1987 upon completion of Catholic high school, with a fresh perspective and a head full of ideas about how to establish the New Utopia on Earth—only to find that the world outside is nothing like we were told it was in the classroom—it is natural that we may tend to lose hope for the future or to fall into despair. Especially at times of transition and new beginnings, "real life" can be a firm contrast against the idealistic musings of young truth-seekers and lovers.

It was in early spring of that year I began to feel the stirrings of powerful forces bubbling up within me, wanting more and more to find a coherent means of creative expression; I was like a pressure cooker that needed to let off steam, or I was going to explode. I was somewhat of an intellectual in my early days (some insist I still am), but like most of my classmates, I was greatly influenced on many levels by the heavies of the Classic Rock music industry, among whom I discovered a fellow poet and constant companion, whose talent would eventually come to validate my budding desire to try my own hand at lyric poetry. His name was Jim Morrison, front man and lead singer for The Doors, and his new book of poetry *The Lords and the New Creatures* (compiled after his death in 1987 and published by Simon & Shuster) was flying off the shelves like hotcakes. My paperback copy had been the first book of poetry I had ever owned, and my mind devoured its pages over and over again until I could remember almost every word by heart. It was not long before I started experimenting with my own style and rhyme, spending hours sequestered in my bedroom listening to my rock and roll, and sometimes even daydreaming my own rise to stardom.

Nevertheless, if I had any aspirations then to be a rock star or celebrity writer, they were soon to be replaced by my more pragmatic need to find out who I really was and who I wanted to become—as well as the need to pay the rent and put food on the table. And so I spent the next two decades uncovering the richest and most potent aspects of myself, through the quiet hours of solitude, as well as with fellow travelers, partners, and explorers on the way. After all, the time when a young man first leaves home and sets out to find himself and his place in the world could perhaps be the most pivotal moment he will ever face in this life—even more decisive than his own wedding day, I suspect. And looking back after a long journey through the wilderness of life, with wider eyes and an opened heart, I am now able to more fully appreciate the challenges I have faced and the obstacles I have overcome; for it is owing to the lessons I have reaped from these experiences that I have become a wiser and better man.

As the road of my life continued to twist and turn, crocheting in and out of the dramas of others I encountered, I came to better understand and accept the layered complexity of my own inherent nature, through my writing and other creative endeavors—including photography, and more recently, the study of herbalism—and have continued to stay current as well as outspoken about the issues and things that really matter to me in life, foremost of which is the increasingly uncertain future of our planetary home, Earth.

So as I embark upon the final stages of this lyrical courtship with the divine, I have chosen a very simplistic structure for my poems, based on the healing system of Traditional Chinese Medicine (TCM), an ancient philosophy which itself is founded upon the sensual interplay of the five natural elements that comprise all life—wood, fire, earth, metal, and water. Thus, I have divided the chapters to correspond with this dynamic alchemical process, recognizing that although each poem tells its story separately and apart from the rest, it is also a vital and integral part of the compilation as a whole. Within this very elastic and symbiotic framework, each piece finds its natural place according to its predominant emotional frequency, thereby providing and sustaining its own harmonic equilibrium in the collection.

But unlike traditional books of its kind, *Taking Tea in the Black Rose* is never finished pouring its light into its readers. Its most enduring and cherished gift is a fragrant unguent for the soul, which it bestows upon anyone who dares to cross the veil-like threshold between what we see with our eyes and what we see with our hearts beyond that.

Over the last several years, *Black Rose* has become my own magic carpet ride, the Jacob's Ladder of my spiritual quest, the philosopher's stone of my magician's sword. It has been my chariot of introspection, allowing me absolute freedom and mobility, in thought and action, capable of transporting me to unimagined worlds on the outer edges of the cosmos with just one thought or meditative glance. But still more than this, I hope that my readers, too, will find a balm of comfort within its pages and grow with life, as I did, to honor and appreciate their struggles as essential pathways by which we all learn to expand and unfold our blessed inner light.

Without a doubt, the twenty-four year process of birthing and now publishing this body of work has been the single most enlightening and visceral undertaking of my life, and so with humble gratitude I warmly acknowledge everyone who has shown the slightest interest in my poetry, or given even a whisper of encouragement to me in earnest; but mostly, I am grateful to you all for accepting my gift just as it is. Also, to the good people at Balboa Press who have so cordially embraced both my work and me, I offer my sincerest thanks and look forward to a great future together.

I found out many times the hard way what can happen to a man when he loses faith and trust in his brothers and sisters, but more importantly when he gives away his own power and stops believing in himself. Oh, the mountains we can summit and oceans we can cross when we believe in our power to succeed and allow others to believe in us, too. For, in order to truly love ourselves, we have to receive as much as we give—and for the generous hearts among us, balance can be a powerful key.

Such are the ways of this living paradise. While I was attending Kalamazoo College, a dear friend gave me a scrap of paper with this simple but eloquent quote written on it—the note read, "The slower you go, the more sunrises and sunsets you'll see." With that same spirit of hope and renewal, I pass his reminder on to you. Take good care of each other and yourself as you travel, respect all life as precious, and leave your destiny to the stars. May our future actions grow from here.

# INTRODUCTION

Life is change—constant and perpetual change. It is an eternal dance, or interplay if you will, between contrasting energetic forces on a three-dimensional, material stage, which brings forth raw, virgin creativity as a consequence. Through history we have devised many names for this great dance of creation, but on the level of interpersonal relations—the very cornerstone of daily human existence, in my view—it can naturally be compared to a courtship, marriage or domestic union, or in the spiritual sense, as "union with the divine", marriage of the small-ess self with the big-ess Self, and so on. It is the willful coming together of seemingly contrary forces for the purpose of composing richer and more advanced forms of matter from the original elements—spiritual alchemy, as some like to call it.

But no matter what metaphors we use to describe it—and modern languages are full of them—life is characterized by the continual converging of our individual paths for the mutual benefit of recognizing and investigating our most hidden fears and manifesting our loftiest dreams, each of us acting in tandem as co-creator with and for the other. In this sense, we are finely polished mirrors reflecting for one another who we really are, versus who we think we are or secretly wish we could be. We accept this reality on some core level without question or curiosity the moment we are born, simply because we know instinctively we can hardly overcome the challenging ordeals or survive the elemental happenings of this capricious world all on our own. No man is an island, or so the saying goes.

Nor is it enough to surrender ourselves or bow unconsciously to the whimsical tides of change without effort or struggle, or even to feel that it must be happening *to* us, inevitably, without our say-so or authority. After all, according to the Law of Attraction, we are both the author and invocator of everything we are now experiencing in this life—in other words, it is all because of me! Setting myself in search of a truly authentic and fiercely independent life, I have spent its latter half immersing myself ever more deeply and consciously in the very personal process of self-examination, becoming bit by bit a wholly present and active participant in the sensual dance of my own shadows and light; not trying to push away the unpleasant parts or keep them under wraps, but rather embracing the wisdom in my misfortunes for the growth it inspires inside me and the matchless beauty in its mysterious yet perfect design. So then, it would seem we draw to ourselves those experiences from which we can glean the most profit spiritually; a lot like we teach others what we most need to learn ourselves. And as the teacher becomes the taught, the pupil becomes his master, all in good time.

In physical duality, we are made up of polarities in all things to some degree, and to believe otherwise (although it is a freewill choice) requires denying oneself the cornucopia of resources we are given each day to expand and to mould our lives anew from the inside out, by shrugging off the toxic and miserable cloak of disappointment and self-pity, and transcending instead the more comfortable and restrictive life that many of our parents and grandparents reasonably wished for us; thereby making way in the field for what we, in our darkest and most personal moments, truly desire for ourselves and our own lives, apart from the needs or desires of the collective.

Each instant we fall into doubt, uncertainty, shame, or indignity—yes those uncomfortable times when we are most vulnerable in our nakedness, humbled in our emptiness, yet most truly alive—each of these gives us a priceless opportunity to replace a tarnished and broken perception of ourselves as the unlovable victim of life's malicious indifference, separate from and at odds with Nature and the rest of life; with a healthier and more coherent perspective, which celebrates the unique personal qualities that honor our wholeness and form the very basis of who we really are, both as individuals and as a species.

Enter Death.

In the West, death of the self is a concept most people grow up learning to fear and eschew at a very early age, widely misunderstood for all the ways the word has been misused since time began, yet passionately embraced by the wise ones of all ages as the glorious gateway by which we can come to genuinely know ourselves, Great Spirit, and the purpose of life itself—that is, should we succeed in releasing what no longer serves us, in favor of self-empowerment and personal freedom, the attainment of which awaits anyone who sets his feet sincerely and courageously on the golden path of initiation. You see, death is something that we experience every day as we awake, stretch, and get up to relieve ourselves in the next room—after we have died to ourselves and our lovers the night before.

However, once we cut through the shroud of mystery and intrigue that death conjures for all of us at some point, we are faced with our pure raw potential as infinitely powerful expressions of consciousness manifesting in a human form full of limitless creative potential, lessened only by the number of days we'll spend in our current physical form. Consequently, we must invariably confront the implicit question of whether to embrace these powers and gifts and walk the rest of the road with our personal power and authority active and intact, or broken and spent from a life in conflict with Nature herself—that living, breathing world embracing our physical body that selflessly supports us in our candid (and often selfish) human pursuits, as well as the natural, yet unseen, passions and tendencies within each of us that we must constantly acknowledge, accept, and incorporate into our individual awareness and being. This is who we are and why we have come here in the first place—we are who we are *because of* our unique experiences, not *in spite of* them. And yet ironically, without death or change, life could never evolve and would eventually cease altogether.

In the same way, the peace we might experience upon the passing of a loved one who has experienced intense or prolonged suffering can perhaps reveal a glimpse of the moment when our life truly makes a lasting change for the better, should we embrace it; but never to such an extent as the contemplation of our own mortality (imminent as it may or may not be) and our basic motivation for starting over fresh that such a candid exploration of one's heart and psyche can reveal. To be in balance and find peace—to truly know yourself—you must come to love yourself.

No matter what belief system you now find yourself a part of—in terms of religion, economics, politics, or the like—if it is founded in limitation of any sort, or in any way restricts your forward motion and personal evolution in this world, then it is safe to say you are out of harmony with the fabric and freedom-loving nature of your very soul. Rest assured, the transforming energies of the world will faithfully expose this dissonance, consciously revealing what it really is—a phantom, a shadow, an illusion craftily created by the ego mind in order to block the light of truth, so as to keep you locked in ignorance and protect you from the very real possibility that you are not merely who you have been up to this point. In this sense, fear arises to indicate an absence or obstruction of the light, which upon more careful scrutiny unmasks itself as pure fantasy, distorting reality faithfully according to *your* non-coherent programming, filters, and masks.

In a sense, the prevailing fear of death among many non-indigenous people in the West is simply a biofeedback control mechanism devised by the subconscious to keep them from venturing too far into their inner landscape and uncovering their own hidden source of light—a very primal energy whose very nature is to burst forth and shower its warmth and love on all life in all directions in equal measure, just like our very own source of light here on Earth—the Sun. Should we choose to accept the fallacy that we are too old, too powerless, or too set in our ways to change, we can be sure that some grand-scale event will eventually come crashing into our tiny lives to remind us of the intrinsic nature of life itself—change. We are all expanding sparks of light, waves of consciousness expressing in matter against an ever changing and expanding backdrop of the world's greatest hopes and dreams all coming into manifestation simultaneously and in synchronicity with one another.

In death, it is tradition in most countries to come together as a family and extended community to celebrate the life and earthly contributions of a loved one whose physical body has come to the end of its earthly wandering and searching. If we are fortunate enough to be able to sit at our loved one's side in their final hours of life, we can't help but feel dwarfed in the awesome power and presence of Source, or be touched profoundly by its amazing capacity to transform every part of life with but the slightest breeze or passing cloud.

Life is a series of coupled events caused by the interactions of two or more bodies in motion. And it is this constant interplay (and at times, friction) between these bodies that gives birth to our greatest achievements and awakenings, thereby feeding the inherent hunger for real change that every soul craves and actively seeks in the world. But what is even more impressive than all these singular characteristics is death's power to bring the light of truth and love to illuminate our darkest and most sorrowful hours.

In this land of ceaseless change, compassion alone has the ability to sever the bonds of hatred, self-doubt, bigotry and conceit, and to proclaim us all for what we truly are, a family of one. This budding realization of our timeless unity—as solid as the stones along every rocky shore, as forceful as the floods in springtime, and as everlasting as the redwood tree that keeps stretching and reaching for the nurturing light above it, century after century—is a symbol of the flowering peace that already resides in us, calling us to nurture it by giving it the proper time and conditions to expand and unfold into the flaming star that each of us, deep down, truly yearns to be.

To die is not to lose, or to fail, or even to set oneself apart. On the contrary, to die is to swim freely in the light of the One that sees all life as equal and dares to love all life free. Perhaps we might consider the examples of the wise messengers and avatars of all faiths and ages, and learn to treat one another as ourselves. But before even this, let us learn to love ourselves fully and to trust that there will always be times when we must ask for another's help, until at last we breathe our final breath.

Man has been taking tea both socially and medicinally for thousands of years, and as a soothing balm for a weary soul or just a nice reward at the end of a long day—hot or iced, with lemon or honey—tea is capable of uplifting the spirit and enhancing our awareness of the divine presence within and all around us, as well as the currents of grace that wander in and out of our lives everyday. The sun rises to greet us each morning like its own cup of tea, brimming with mystery and excitement for both the curious and the passionate alike.

Throughout the countless experiences of my own life (good, bad, and not-so-pretty), I've found myself becoming the crucible itself in which the sacrament of creation is performed, the once unbearable tension between shadow and light now finally resolved by my newly awakened eyes and inner calm. So I strongly advise taking each day as it comes, sip by sip, savoring the aroma and enjoying its color and flavor, never forgetting to fully accept one another in the process—not in spite of our differences, but because of them.

New worlds are conceived through the power of the poet's plume, and the serenades of sweethearts are what craft them into form. May the spirit of wisdom and charming affection enfold you all the days of your life, both in this world and beyond its azure shores.

# Chapter 1

# *Forest*

# *Spark of Seduction*

Just beneath
the grave I used to
rock myself to sleep
I journeyed with iron wings
even to infinity's edge
at last
to bring to light
the simplest reason for waking
Being formed from
a formless folly
I
felt my flame flee
into vast caverns
beneath the twisted roots
of the Juniper tree
primal life-giver of countless limbs
wholesome, full of vim and vigor
in a timid past
presently diseased
by time's wicked neglect
they genuflect in accord
with a broader will
dangling desperately
fingering fossils for rhyme
perpetrating a crime my comrades
stood guard against for centuries
But the lords have told me
not to delay
for surety sleeps not near
nor yet is there any sense in fear
while precious Caroline trails behind
these moonlit shadows
weighing the morning against the night
invisible to men

but through the needle's eye
she waits for me
there
on the other side of daybreak
For a brief moment I surrender
seven miles
short of the green grass
free-falling through the well
wondering if it could last
or have I been
like a babe fast asleep
sucking the nectar
from the lily
all along

20 June, 1991

# *On Disappointment*

## *(Man's Impish Need for Approval)*

"Desperately seeking just that special someone to
reject, ignore, or horribly despise me
to nourish the self-sabotaging snares set by
a decrepit mind diseased down deep inside me."

It's not so much a gift for reading the future
as much as an acuity for reckoning with the past

Between Father Sky and Mother Earth
I am the fear of being
and the courage to be victorious
ambition, the most crooked desire of all

Stop pretending to know
what is best for someone else
when your prime challenge is knowing
what is best for yourself

I am taunted by the fever in my veins
to smother your sweet red lips again
so I store my treasures up in heaven's chest
and leave demons to merry with men

At times you may get a little dirty when
you're trying so hard to come clean
I point my blade to the center of the rose
mastermind of the circle enclosing me
I collapse alone on this oaken threshold
pause for brief reflection—
am I just another fool for love?

After all I'm but a fraction of who
I always thought I was
a cynical spark-stone ignites my ire
once demonized, now dissolved as
desire for union eclipses the ambiguity
of my worldly concerns, implores me
to alter my present course
as the river of time trickles on

And so I live out the remainder of my days
hoping that we might one day be wed
at the end of this wave's deliberate delays
we're just a couple of cowardly lions
who've conveniently misplaced their roars

A lifetime's disappointment has got me
wondering about you lately—defeat
has never been my strongest suit and
Futility's this lonely guy I never seem to shake

When folks get to talking will you stand up for me, or hush?
"I'm sorry" after the fact tends to beg an embarrassing blush

Mortal words would only reinforce
the floating veil this side of magic's love
and hatred's last punch for pride
finds my weakness a most natural glove

Worlds fall to ruin when we idle along
leaving the slippery slope to servants
and the hard work left undone
But now with wheels moving faster
and doorways lining up towards the sun
we pulse with the heart of the infinite
our lives back-burnered for the
"sake of the greater good"

From this craggy edge on moonlit shores
I soothe over my grief but never tinker with remorse
and awaken to find nothing visibly amiss—all memory
erased from the previous night's bliss
A new blue planet hovers unseen beneath us
tickling our tender new toes as a clean
identity slips seamlessly into place

Have faith in your adventure, not fear
for pride proceeds to malice and wicked revenge
Self-praise and hubris will only whittle you down
so forgive the fears in your heart by then

Spring 2007

# *My Heart Shattered*

My heart has shattered
into a thousand tears for you
your shrieking voice still loitering
around the core of my obsession
my bloody bones rattle onward to oblivion
carving deep into your plush vulnerability
like a mighty sword that once drew kings
and disciples to their knees in shame
I am sorely aware of their innuendoes
about women and men I once knew
my senses tattered perhaps, yet always
attuned to their petty intent
suspicion is surely now spent in the
cobwebs of my juvenile mind
I am vast in my own sweetness sipping
candied youth from a straw as the
world swirls madly about in wild abandon
blasting heads of all man's kind

22 January, 2010

## *(Semper as) Ox House Humper*

Advancing archers abandon arrows
Blazing brilliance born between
Cathartic crises calm calamity
Defending damage defiantly
Escape espoused epiphany
Fettered fold, fecundity

11 August, 2006

# *Restless Angel*

We used to laugh aloud and rattle
our bones to the romance of the night
in love our youth would never end
we were countless and for each other
we'd never hesitate our fragile honor to defend

Teen-age vagrants, we crowded the city streets
revealing a host of vital mysteries
in every second step a new order disclosed
but shedding our innocence we were alone
the hermit's lamp the profane exposed
will shine no more but in the poet's stone
where the rain against the sidewalk beats

As if in a dream the doorway to freedom
stood open for me like that fateful day
my mother in tears first called me by a name
it was the night I met Melissa under
a shower of stars stashed from our sight
and for the confidence that came from
a lonely lion's heart we felt somehow
still curiously to blame

Until we were married I was a
true reckless type, staying out for hours
pitting myself against the shadows of the night
and though my routine seldom changed
I was forever caught without warning
holding a dying candle to those dauntless figures of light
　　　　Never had a mannish boy seemed so lonely
　　　　Never had a mannish boy felt so blue

Like the rebirth of spring, Melissa gave me
immunity from the frozen stream

cloaked in a sweetness my lips have never known
I soared in a sky by vultures never flown

My love for her grew to such lengths
I hardly noticed the quickening disease
this illness I'd lived with since childhood, I knew
it would one day bring me to my knees
But for the moment she gave me unjaded love
an appreciation for the sublime, it seemed that
falling in love with her I was learning
to love for the very first time

Now gazing into a portrait against
the blush of a vesper sky she says,
"There is love and love, in everything
there is the serpent and the dove."

From that day forward I prayed upon waking
that my life never fall void of distinction
to be of the advantage of felicity forewarned
and as a daily rite her bedside with scarlet
    blossoms be perpetually adorned

She could sweep against misfortune and
never cause a spark of friction
well read from a lifetime on the golden road
she'd speak in subtle contradiction

Then somehow she found a blessing in my dying
diamonds in the sweat beads on my withering corpse
as I for the last time fatefully awoke, I longed
to feel the cool breath of morning on her lips

Despite my good lady's faithful affection
her courage of heart besides
she was no match for the demon inside me
now coiled and ready to strike

I was shivering fiercely when
the midnight messenger arrived
though I was deaf to the bells
that rang in front of his call
with purpose and will he rushed in
winked with an eye no less contrived
and in a blinding flash of certainty
pinned my shadow to the wall
    Never had this mannish boy felt so helpless
    Never had he wanted so much to be free

Melissa held my cold and trembling hand
a look of disbelief behind her eyes
she had shown me such beauty when I was blinded
and in a miracle of faith she realized

"It makes no difference," she whispered,
"if you stand or if you fall; but that you recognize
the splendor and harmony of the journey
and hear the beauty in the law."

As I rise the stars are my confessions
though they be faint against these city lights
alive in an instant, even brief, hand in hand
we peer through veiling clouds, then out of sight
Call it faith or unconscious belief
I salute life's fantasy so far beneath

Winters wait only for the changing of the leaves
life is love and so as strange
How gracefully we fly
when we in happiness weep
How deeply we dream
    when we rock ourselves to sleep

21 September, 1991

“I’d say even Vanity could exercise a
little restraint as she goes strutting about
in front of nature’s mirror of remorse.”

Today a house mouse is my demon,
and his name is Scrutiny.

Beg pardon.

20 April, 2009

# *Weaving*

I am lost and caught up
in this world confined
to this foursquare vagrant's prison
alone but for the dreamy
feather-like flutter of
your tender fingers, weaving
together all these stray
strands bunged up in my heart
you are the web I created with you
it wraps me round and round
keeping me tangled in your
shadowy intrigue, always
reaching, yet only a lick of
your cosmic innocence
is left on these cracked
pink lips, after so much blood
they know no more
than to mumble absolute
foolishness while we chase
one another in the streets
with sharp knives
in defense of your honor

31 December, 2009

# *Moving in Place*

Where lines are drawn let no man
look into the eye of love and live
for death looks not wisely, nor with more brevity
than the emerald from which the tablets speak
on him, who for the sake of his own
be unmindful of the desires of a friend and
when to stop giving, and how not to spend

The evening bears witness with a watchful eye
she sees lovers part and others start
along their futile way to gather the fresh
promise of the day and nothing more

The birthright of one fertile seed shivers
like dominion rooted in the somber scalp of night
leaning and reaching toward the docile April sun
she holds a prism to the daylight, separates
her colors, and swirls them into black

Her sister, Dawn, the process reverses
to bring the rainbows back
her confidence hesitates a second
but once engaged, drips like candied sentiment
from her lips and wakes me from these
sleepy fields that never bloom or yield

Her father once told me not to ride within these lines
but now I fear the time I can spare is too brief
to admit what I'm honestly feeling
to learn the sonata my heart longs to play
and dupe the darkness my mind's been dealing
come what may, come what may

And so I say all good things, like fine wine, take time
so take a sip, step back and focus
what a thing to perceive when a prism
shatters the daylight, mixing the colors into night

It's hard so far from home to understand why
the two of us together is still the two of us alone
truth plays no stranger when you're living
by the sword—one eye watches east
one watches west, while four guard the gateway
to the place that's the best

It's here I find with sinless surprise
a coffer full of yesterday's treasures
a ship of dreams I bequeathed to myself
still afloat behind an old man's eyes

Ahead of his goad we sail unsuspecting
into the Great Unreality
leaving behind what cowards
sign with grief and misery

Is there nothing more intriguing
or suspicious than a sermon
delivered by a martyred saint
or the prophetic one-liners of a
poet or warlock or lawyer in love?

This sublime wisdom of a morning dove
dedicated as it were from me to you
now and through the twilight hours
as you converse with angels
choose carefully your stance
and when at last you find the notion
won't you come dance with me again?

7 March, 1992

# *Crickets in the Misty Rain*

I'd do almost anything to silence
the howling winds of our astral mind
that cluttered space between daily
life here and beyond, a canopy of
chaos of every earthly kind

I believe in the power of love to shift
shapes from music in the heavens
to broadcast their graceful sounds and patterns to
every corner of cosmic gloom, and surround
me sweetly in my super-conscious drift

This planetary life is a balance of exchanges
of money, philosophies, and personal effects
a series of hopscotching waves on a turbulent sea
they canvass life with painful duress and tug
at the heartstrings of friends we'd neglect

At one time from my sun-power I entertained
holding others bound to this space
but with each new piece of this puzzle in place
the cold moon's reflection reminded me—
it was liberation from my own hell I sought

Coyote's tricks and nocturnal chatter had signed
my name to their bottom line and through
the chorus of the nighttime air barked
a curious reminder that life's magical spirit lies
closer than my breath or weakening pulse
"Why still dost thou seek without, my friend?"

19 August, 2006

# *You're Missed, in Silence*

## *(Tu me manques mais ne dis rien)*

The beauty of life
as with the blooming of a rose
unfolds so tenderly
infused by its rhythmic aroma
we celebrate our daily bread
its sweet fragrance the passing of time

The numbers and rhyme mean nothing, 4 or 24
both our lives have been
shaped by a gentle bond, a love of
which we both too seldom speak
It's there—sometimes it stays hidden
cast out with its camouflaged source
far away from home as we know it
in search of warmth and mutual love

Now you and I stay always attached
bonded by the curious distance between us
cuddled and caressed by those
tingly feelings not just a look,
a gesture, or a smile can describe

The silence is safety for everyone
the speaker, the thrill seeker is the one
who takes a chance at truly living
peeking through this devilish veil of time

Our love is never ending because
it is ageless; it was never born

Je t'aime, Papouné
4 May, 2001

# Unapportioned Giving

Impulsed again and again
to put my pen to the tablet
of life's most courteous destiny
by nameless shadowy figures
of a neutral and unaffected design
plucked like the harp strings of fantasy
by slivery fingers of sunlight
so buoyant in the smile of
an unfamiliar calm

They move me to my challenge
and show the way to the
door of gratuitous instruction
from this hopeful light of regeneration
I bow to the folds of fruitful form
and in my humblest reflection I confront
the ghost of my past, standing speechless
beneath ripe contagious starlight

And for this I come now again
not as pupil with eyes wide and awake
but pursed in compassion and quietude
knowing well the turbulent waters
you'll still have to cross
Poised in readiness at the last glint of
daylight, you emerge from the ocean's
mayhem whirling tossed

Amaryllis, Lady of Paradise
and sweet fragrant lotus in bloom
birther of the vernal thaws that
clear away all fears and doubt
the winter snows concealed
all life is uplifted and restored by

your smile, all harmony in perspective
all crossroads by Jove revealed

The taught become the teachers through
cycles of heritage we've handed down
Plumes of a raging child's restlessness beat
like wings from my smoldering scalp
yet the golden locks of my fairest advice
are by devotion and peaceful principle crowned

I am drawn according to the new fashion of my
loveworks—I live now in this moment cloaked
forever in the glory of an unwritten name
I even erected a stone tomb last night
in honor of your silent escaping
the hot-white sparks of the turret's flaming
peak still fresh in my tired mind
they tickle my saltcellar's seduction with
a golden harvest our calloused hands have grown
I blink! and with a curious pause
organic life bursts forth once more
from the flint of the earth a single flash
with hushed civility lights aglow, and all
around me stand in garments newly sewn

For Awen
20 March, 2007

## Daydreaming Our Beauty's Disguise

winter's wicked wheat is well on its way to
the grain silos and markets in town
spinach crops are sore-spotted and rotten
our heartland is in decay, its buildings crumbling down

in step our local farmers chasing three blind mice
who've run off with the top-secret cheese but what
a shame they can't believe all the grace they've received
showers equally on us all like the breeze

our marshlands moan with a stench of heavy metal death
    fluoridated pools of propaganda and liquid disguise
while doctors, chemists and government boards
throw smoke and mirrors in our rose-colored eyes

these same tricksters assure us that it's for our own good
    that without them we would never survive, but
vaccines it seems have candy-coated our dreams
and so diminished the course of our lives

we've poisoned Emerald City in our ignorance
    with our parental minds in disarray, attempting to
shelter our children from every evil known to man
while they run out of time and safe places to play

so as you hurry off to your office job or drown yourself
in a sea of distractions for the day, I'll just mull
around here and hang old pictures on my wall
tuning out the daily buzz of what my critics all say

pursuits of power and money turn quite naturally to greed
when the light of love loses its earthly appeal
if in the end a lasting peace you seek, with grace
you'll find it on your next turn around this wheel

our ship of fools is sinking in its darkness, and fast
    you've been left all alone at your post for a reason
    with the freedom of choice you were gladly given
you chose a life of hypocrisy and treason

the truths they left out of your history books
    like the lies they've typed in their place
    spell disaster for sure for the emerging world
should rational thought be kept out of this race

so each morning when you wake up, give thanks
    count your every blessing one by one
then praise life for your power to choose and
keep reaching for the transforming sun

every action or inaction passes a torch to its mother
    as a father his beliefs to his new-born son
    so our days may be numbered accordingly
but our lifetimes all roll into one

good morning, dear brothers and sisters—
    now good night.

20 September, 2006

## *Life Springs Internal*

When you live the truth you glean
from the joys and labors of your journey
you inspire and enrich all living forms

This we do simply for our love of service
and our service to Love, besides

10 March, 2011

# Chapter 2

# *Desert*

# *Scarlet Sacrifice*

When again will the lion lie down with the lamb?
No more shall a master dictate the limits
of his power by some artistic fancy or whim
Within these shores we are free
persons and states, wholly sovereign as
the lights dancing in the night sky
We seek leadership from those with
kind affection and respect for all life
likewise, for the common agreements
passed down from our Fathers and theirs
We admit only those who faithfully
abide the consent of the governed—
men and women of honor and right action
fierce protectors of the divine rights of our people
A flowering cosmic brushfire is sizzling
in the hearts of our weary race but not until
the old guard is replaced will the one
tribe of many know release from the
stranglehold of social and fiscal servitude
as we together face down our
Godzilla of greed and selfish waste
Then, seated at last at the round table of
brotherhood, all in mutual purpose renewed
One alone lies down with love as a
fading hour unmasks a treacherous few

3 July, 2011

# *With Pure Intent*

Love calls so restlessly from
across foul distance and
time's auspicious mistakes, still
no less a lie ever sat before you
than this leathery hide of mine
encasing mechanical reflex of
sinews and skeletal decay
it smolders with an
unforgettable stench
beneath the ashes of
another fictitious war
winter's sanctity concealed
estranged from its radiance by
infinite folds of comfort food
and criminal aerosol impurity
my broader ambition was to scour
these layers of hollow silence to
unearth the gem of my desire
Alas! the verdant blush of springtime
in youth poisonous upon my brow
now taunts my aims to full reproach
last night's passion entombed in defeat
still blazes with the promise of liberty
yet beyond the glory of shadowless days
I hang these rags on a rusted nail
a place my sandals once called home
finally by sweet suffering revealed
and in crushed velvet vacancy
I attain matrimony with me

1 November, 2006

## Chronic Lament

I concentrate a gaze upon my
bedroom wall, an off-white canvass
spotted with fears—should the future
embrace a harlot with just one kiss
then disappear behind her laughter
never quite sure what she's after
until next year?

She paves the road with choices
trades the morning for premature
twilight, her purpose to quicken
the pace of time, then meets her lover
in the rain for just one night, the two
together content, but saddest of all
their days should fall without notice like
the sour breath of a chronic lament

Each day disguises the same sacred word
to verbal penetration immune like a rolling vein
or a reluctant virgin, laughing and
sobbing in one voice, we spell it and
speak it the same front to back
yet between those symbols
shrouded under a veil of broken light
an emperor labors for centuries to construct
a palace in honor of his mistress, sensuous
now sleeping she dreams of that castle
in the sky, fragile to the childish minds
of men, until the delicate egg begins to crack

She races back to rekindle a
world that failed her, a warm zephyr
sprays from her lips, a helix rising from its
conception like the spiral breeze that fills

a conch shell with sounds of the sea
a double union on a beach that never ends
and thanks to you I don't feel so blue
every now and then; Viola from the rooftop, or
a misguided cloud spot, cries a widow's sigh and chants
for the death of a love, a would-be chronic lament

How noble and foolish are they
who will try their love again
for man is the cornerstone of humanity
and wades to his knees in waters that
run red with mystic blood, stalking
the child who would avenge his brother's
death; he would never beg your pity or even
an admission of the fears you fester
just a little sympathy and a blindfold
stitched with the loose threads of stories
tragically left untold of a brother who once
bugled the dawn upon the morning dew, only sweetness
and no fiery fury of abuse from his tongue:

"I regret that I cannot, I will not see you go—
for the lamp of wisdom is lit from within
like daylight lost in its own web of shadows,
and what a cold night it is without you!"

Ghosts disperse and spirits rise
suicide, my child, met me naked
in the rain last night, so give me no
thorns with my victory, please
no categorical decrees, just a soldier's
heart inflamed with promises
his sensitivities spent and if
I weren't such a coward I'd leave a
farewell at the door again; then to have no one
and nothing but a dusty dream, a love
I could have shared, maybe I should never
have dared to court destruction, it seems,

like an eager moth who flirts too cordially with the flame
for as such I can never sing the obvious ode
to my lover's chronic lament

24 January, 1992

## *A Most Sacred Affair*

O Great Birther of the universe
whose sensual, silent embrace
sets a pace of constancy to
these salt-filled seas
the circling stars, the ever aging
moons that circle the halls of heaven
with but a whirling whisper and
penetrate this silent daybreak
surrounding me

I humbly pour my heart
into your overflowing hands
I am captured by your beauty
sleeping so comfortably behind
veils of shimmering light and
translucent traces of great
love affairs that once inspired
mystic poets and Wall Street
banksters alike

I crawl to your doorstep
a dusty beggar at midnight
with the hope of catching
one fleeting glimpse of
your most sensuous charms
I linger like a nervous voyeur
at your garden gate while
you brush the feathery
locks of gold dust back
away from those mysterious
almond-shaped eyes

Then I creep like a schoolboy
out of class without a hall pass

and scamper back to my
rustic quarters where suspicion
keeps my cache from covetous spies
these morsels of memory I keep
wrapped in velvet folds till
at last I am called to expose
your treasures in the calico
radiance of a lioness moon
this fairy's tale hopelessly doomed
unless with craft and subtlety I can
pull you down from your throne
I plant a single kiss in
the nape of your neck
to reveal my true passion to you
and as my covenant of love until
the day in death we must part

In perfect form, Ra's golden boat stretches
catlike across my marble floors, finding
the two of us entwined in silent sweetness
embracing one another in life
as many times in death before
like a meadowlark your voice
enchants me to my weary bones
I am stillborn to the world of man
as if all this had been only fantasy
and these nocturnal wanderings
through the starry seas a mere figment
of my lost and broken mind

Now as I rub the sleep from my eyes
I rise to greet the ghostly
image of her singular grandeur
vanishing like the morning dew
She blows me a kiss from
her phantom veil and promises
to return to me again soon

I step outside to drink in the early
morning air, and standing there,
I pause for but a twitch to reflect
on the midnight love affair
she and I were blessed to share
recollecting visions of my every
dream come true
her virgin beauty and genius
inscribed in my sacred heart
now but a legacy for a tender few

8 August, 2007

# *Front Row Seat to God*

Bumblebees chant the Icaros for me
      tapping codes in the mosaic of my molten mind
tip-toeing breathlessly from your maiden's milk
they gather clues from my inner ear's design

the stone beneath my skull emits a fragrance
of spiced persimmon and chestnuts
I've tuned in to something spectacular
miraculous—at worst a sublet home

I sip your sinful blasphemy through fragmented breath
my nostrils licked by the charity of passing horseflies
as the decadent buzz of the Amazon gives me certitude
and this priceless front row seat to God

For Madame Aya
9 October, 2005

## *Certainly Not I*

Certainty is the taproot of ancient
man's mammoth self-deception
his densest and most stubborn lie
the seething core of his vanity, pride
across the millennia, his self-importance
has led to terrific aggression against his
own parents, siblings and home
nearing total estrangement from himself
he now seeks a fateful, bitter end

O modern man, give up your
trivial pursuits of surety and
throw caution to the ever-shifting winds
they alone are promised their day
but we, the useless humors of a
collapsing age now gone seriously astray
forefront in our forgetfulness
even our compass has lost
linkage with the loving light
of its true north, delay

The haystacks moan for your childish seeking
whistle as the dance of night and day
dispenses its own versions of silver and gold
they cannot help you now
nothing can, O future man
embrace your ignorance and whip
the lion from its insulated den
wipe the crust of the ageless sleep
from your eyes, O guardians of
pure nothing and let the magical
light of freedom's dawn pour in

30 June, 2010

# *10 Minutes Worth Repeating*

Speak of love at first sight to the average man
he'll relate through the eyes in his head
but offer sight to a blind man for ten minutes alone
he'll share a lifetime of loneliness instead

Not even he is immune to a love such as this
though he sees with a queer eye indeed
unscarred by destruction and human ugliness
his sight is of a nobleman's breed

Through daily hope he savors the prospect
of having his full sight restored, but to see
beauty snatched like a thief in the night
such luxury this poor heart can't afford

Courage, a gander with uncharmed reflection
through the well that hides deep in his soul
he's face-to-face with the child he once knew
before his refined adult senses took hold

So in the interest of fairness, count your blessings
and to your curses, a wink and a nod
give your heart to the girl who blushes before you
and leave tomorrow's creations for God

When Cupid aims his bow, the planets stand down
while the whole world slips wordlessly away
the only thing left, his beloved's silhouette
and a drumbeat that stands in his way

On the eve of deployment, his preacher advised,
"Son, know your enemy—his color, tongue, and breed."
The soldier turned back, "With all due respect, Sir,
Love's all the advice I shall need."

War and love are not too dissimilar
each one's result the same in the end
like a switch off to on for the animal mind
they awaken the hidden breath of men
The death of a child by irrational war
a mother's injustice, an unrightable wrong
her prayers, we'd all do well to remember
add up to but a blind soldier's song

4 November, 2006

## *Lynx's Lost Remark*

We golden seeds of potential
from timeless specks of sand and dust
evolve into our diamond forms fresh
out of the Creator's grandest living dream
Great Champion of innovation, all in my time
I glorify your name and nature for giving
me these precious organs and
the will to breathe forth the potent
desire of my conscious creation

Daily grains of wheat and wisdom fall
from my lips in pure devotion to you
singing praises to your perfection as we pass
through this dense prelude to silence
challenging the tight grip of destiny
with the coal-hearted blackness of nowhere
we color the night's cool embrace
with the spectral blanket that is
our dawn, our noontime meal
and the broken stories of our journey
we share with our beloved and unseen kin
around a crackling fire to mark
the close of our day
Selah

Come to celebrate the mystery of the desert sands
swirling in madness inside the sacred hourglass
keeping measure and pace with our evolving
all together unfolding with puny pageantry till
on my mark they slip cat-like out of sight
past the drowning emptiness of the needle's
unforgiving eye, we parade our war
machines through the streets on May Day
the longest day slips away without apology

as every kernel of potential
every spark of your yearning surrenders
in intimate fulfillment to my heart on fire

All lust and wickedness are revealed in time
but pure love remains in crystal light
dancing like a wandering gypsy down the
camel's road to freedom
behind his Mona Lisa smile a great
cat's mystery to the wise remains untold
of necessity and ancient obedience to law
but shines in beauty beyond measure
cloaked by eons of wind and thirst
his polished perfection grins with liquid
silver and electric gold in our absence

21 August, 2006

## The Creative Science of Destruction

So, is it by grace that I peek so
candidly into my most forgotten self
a snapshot stolen as I turned away
or with a potent particle of mind so cleverly
crafted in its form and image, disguised
as an innocent hello to a curious world
a peasant's portion got left behind like
breadcrumbs for the starlings
thoughtfully planted to feed the
creeping hunger of our homecoming
while neighbors from netherworlds chatter
across the ethers to one another
like young girls on their
telephones after school
honestly, no sweeter gift could I receive
than another hour of playtime
in your brown-throated breeze

19 June, 2009

# *Give Up a Devil's Due*

Recognizing your beauty
in everything seals my case
to be sure or still unclear
I rise above the fall
past temptation's harness in
the belly of the serpent of life
swallowed by the slippery
snake whole, practically raw
like your son's own mystery soul
beaten by the uncaring wildness
of my own reflection
as yet undecided but
deliberately more awake
this time I will not follow you
back to your vanishing past
at last I have some sanctuary
in my airy empty nest
I am instantly beheaded in
the presence of your grace
the acid of animal ambition
chars my mindless whims, purges
itself at will from the inner organs'
foul and gaseous condition
in sparkling lunchtime reflex
I fall upon your priceless infinity
the bad, the good, the not so pretty
all standing at attention
like an army of giddy school kids
in a deliciously impish light

My faith restores pre-destiny's
delicate allurement
captured by an ancient wherefore
in the wink of a one-eyed witch

I am slathered by your bashfulness
enslaved by your erotic intrigue
concealed in a star that shines
forever upon my forehead
and yet I tie myself to thee
thus speaks the master therein
moodiest mark of a man
"sin"—no more divisive a
word could there be
four swords crossed in truce
not merely a lie for noble intent

It carries a unique light for each of us
yet it's the same in every way
I've been rolling this stone for so long
now I can't feel anything at all
and though these howling
winds still haunt me
they tell a trite but tragic tale
of a breathtaking innocence I once despised
messenger of death, fearless transformer
of the flow, fluidity, then flight
released by blind abandonment
upon impure flesh and bones
beneath a secret canopy of leaded glass
we are swallowed whole, squeezed through
the entrails of the great devourer of light
As I lean over for another sip of
chamomile tea, the time on
the alarm clock reads 11:11
and then it all stops

17 August, 2007

# Miracle Minuet

And they say love is the
deadliest illusion of them all . . .

Her heart by constant infidelity
scarred, she wonders how it
could ever come to this
and how often we miss those
things that mean the most
when we to triviality toast
and to the over-zealous bride
I, too, have hurried to hide
from all the games and countless lies
that complicate our lives and
leave us mad before our time

Nothing of darkness exists without light
exposure and rapture
a harmony of halves but enemies to all
and to none a silent past
well, only one . . .
the one I know and love
in my soul and in between
the measured moments where
the serpent courts the dove

Should the voice of prophecy
one day come true
may the dream we seek be
handsomely designed for two

8 November, 1992

# (Ecstasy of Sweet) Surrender

As a loyal hound who only knows
to heel by his master's side
I pursue with blind obedience
the quiet kiss of my beloved bride

Lured by the sugared serenity in
her soft unspoken song I am
trapped in a web of bewilderment
formed of her veils of dazzling light

She is the path that leads to my remembrance
of a time when everywhere I'd belong
she is clothed in rapture like none other
I could have dreamed in this desert of night

Now drunk on images of my lurid union
with her youthful innocence, I respond
faithfully to your silent call from
the emptiness of the great beyond

Assuredly lost, yet your devoted son
I feel my way blindly back home
loaded with the treasures she and I have spun
through these shadows of sweet oblivion

22 August, 2009

## At Peace, like Fire and Ice

A flock of geese gander by in majestic form
attuned high above to the whispering trees
they carry a message of victory from the ancients
who have come to see the wars on Earth cease

"This is not a class reunion, Dear Ones,
no need to don your warrior gear
gang warfare is a line for the history books
and has lost our nod around here.

"You were drafted into strife so sinister
you cannot fathom or believe, but still
you sweat and toil to co-create what
we all know you can never achieve."

Buried within me burns a lust so wicked
I do but wish I could relieve an itch
I can't quite reach, my frozen heart
ignites the match, like fire to ice I snap
knowing surely that we're the ones
they must so callously deceive

I'm just a soldier of circumstance
stabbing his pen into a notebook's crease
a coward's way out of this insanity
in the hope of finding some short reprieve

Despite our prayers, you're touched by destiny
yet force a smile upon your sleeve
while you wander in a toxic wasteland
we somehow know you'll never leave

Your heart must be your sanctuary
it dries the mist from the morning breeze and
illuminates the tragic disconnect between
hearsay and the truth your inner self conceives

31 August, 2006

# Chapter 3

# *Valley*

# *Dying Embers*

In my ashes cold awaits you
no acquaintance or recollection of me
no lasting guilt
there is part of me that hides
but a fading smile
the sorrow of my passing
a hope that lingers a while and whispers
in your heart adorned with mirth
my embers cooling swiftly
beneath this smoky evening haze
our joys adrift in my remembrance as
the morning sun dreams up another day
In my ashes there is no part of me that cries
for in this body void of feeling
I've concealed a crippled space divine
with fortune renewed and senses weary
my inner angel conjures a
spark of laughter that lingers a while
yet never leaves my side
In my ashes there is no part of me that dies

3 April, 1999

# *Patience of the Pelican*

Light hearts flutter
with the downy-filled
flapping of your wings
no one beneath you
nor above you
a half-dozen newborn
chicks close beside you
Caressed by your ceaseless
maternal surrender
they chirp the patient
song of blissful escape
nestled cozy and deep
in the gentle heaving of
your swollen bosom
my all-time safest place
Here entrained hearts echo
with the very ebb and flow
of the groaning tides
marking the rhythmic fluidity of
one life to the next
as the wings of an albatross
aloft in gossamer skies
Certainly we are guided
all through our growth
by the clanking of resonant poles
man's urgent fidelity meets
woman's generous expectancy
while young pelicans shuffle
through tropical sands

Peace and Aloha
carry us all of our days
through this journey
on eternity's breath

9 November, 2007

## *Impossible Dream*

To them my life seems full of hope
    of dreams for the future
of eternal happiness in a world of opportunity.
But what I see can only be explained
    by my experiences, good and bad,
my eyes blinded by their effects.

To them I seem rebellious
    in rejecting their gifts and concern
in wanting to create a possibility to succeed.
But my methods are not always clear.
It is I who fail to explain why I must leave
why I cannot accept their dreams as my own.

To them I seem insincere
    in wanting to establish my independence
in finding freedom in solitude.
How long can I remain an image of their fantasies?
Is it I who must change to suit you?
And how many times did you change for me?

To you I seem a static image
    "encumbered by the pressures of daily living,
distracted by a boy's need for attention."
To me I'm a wanderer searching the world for a dream
    awakening from a paralyzing slumber
and yearning to set myself free.

18 March, 1987

# (The Hero Dreams) Wished Away

Did you ever meet Southtown's forgotten hero
who'd strut about in hats and high-heeled shoes
never at a loss for love to throw around
he yielded to no one, but could not choose
from the numbers and odds, who was to win
next week's championship fight

All day he buries his nose in books
on everything from Danish history to prose
and from the fantasies his life construes the works
of his own heroes, Baudelaire and Proust

The vagrants stayed content scrounging
for food stamps in the lost-and-found
while he spent hours at home
tirelessly waiting beside the phone
only to hear the rubbish of
yesterday's poorly written news . . .

CEREMONIES OF DARK RACE BEGIN AT NOON—
WE MUST BE READY!

And in that instant
a snapshot in the voyeur's eye
the shadowy planet against
the racing clouds is stilled

A draft stirs the black
breath of a closet mind
swirling the leaves to stillness
in the eddies of time
Daniel ferrets the reason for his return
to reclaim the daylight
and still our concern

All cameras focus on the decrepit trunk
tucked away in the farthest corner of the room
where Daniel, as a cocky youth, had leaked
the contents to reporters, but not with impunity
as one might assume

In the garden below the orchestra ready their ascent
while we with hushed apprehension await
the showering serenade—and Daniel watching so shyly
all his money spent, a sack of rags and bones
fans the four winds at his back, unknowing
he beards the lion in his den

Light cancels night in the wink of an eye
burnt deep in his eyes the reflection of sky
a rumor steals mouse-like through chattering reeds
as a rough-feathered raven with fervor jets by

Spanish moss hangs limp from age-old pines
where spirit-fire spits from gnarled roots
climbs cautiously like mercury to cardinal heights
and with ravenous jaws meets the
oppressive decay of long-muted seeds

Four-squared and double are they, these
children of light, velvet petals of the fire-flower
flashing sweet inspiration in the streets
like criminals stealing through the starry night

Up in the attic Daniel stands reeling
under the weight of a cypress wood cross
he clears his throat to greet a wanderer from afar
plucking a message from an acoustic guitar

He approaches, chanting dryly,
"What falls from the wagon is lost.
I feel like a child, with yet no teeth to chew, so
to success let us drink and make everything well."

Here in the polluted catacombs
freely as the lizard roams
the child inside crawls naked
out of dampened decay

A wild wind echoes through
sanity's deepest throes
and closes the door on this
hero dreams wished away

Now in the single glint where matter
strokes his dreams, a thief at the crossing
snatched his memory, exhuming the corpse
of a secret that until now lay quietly untold
He left one regret behind and nothing more,
"I could have found solace in silver
all this time I've been mining for gold."

Danny-boy calls out for comfort, when Clarity
with ragged tongue cuts in,
"That which supports me must also resist me."
He raises his finger to his
lower lip, resigns to sleep alone

When the last thread of civility
has been stretched beyond repair
a live wire melts your senses, leaving
your emotions stripped and bare

I am a man like any other, I've secrets
I fight desperately to hide, yet undressed
to gratify this panel of judges, the slightest
breath my memory will abide

Now I've returned in vagabond rags, it's hard
to say just who and where I've been
or how I came to be so worn and out of touch
for surely death nods but does not consent

And who's to be king of the world today, Dan?
Can his merits appease him, and what kind of man
could with his solitary might
bring Goliath to his knees?
Only a dying peasant untamed
by the history war's winners write

And who again will dare to
lift the lid off of the night?

23 November, 1991

Expectation is the forefather of
disappointment
and as equally delicious

4 May, 2011

# *Incompletely Yours*

As this stairway I descend I kiss
the glance we chanced to share
and if I asked, would you have cared why
when we met I turned away and
to your best friend heard you say
you're a little lonely now and then?

The question rings again in the tin rain
against my rooftop, dancing a calypso
to the rhythm of my wheels
In these times of vacancy she keeps me
running through dampened streets
her restless bloodhounds at my heels

Sweat-soaked and out of breath I
arrive at familiar shelter, slip
between the gateway and the holly hedge
where the earth is sanctified and lies
breathing at my feet
Her rib cage heaving
as I tip-toe in silence inside this
all-consuming ecosphere of
chalk dust, leathery jumpsuits and
guaranteed death by sticker shock

The night air is deafening, it closes
out all sounds, except one voice whispering
wordlessly through moistened lips
turning heads with wax fingers
cutting the silence in two, it renders
my wisest thoughts absurd

An Edmonton wind wraps a chill
around the churchyard, plants a blockade
against the spring armada approaching
Lost and insecure, we toss flowers
as we wander through fields of polished stone
Ribboned bouquets sing crimson by day
calico in the moonlight they decay and
sift through the cracks in the old
abbey walls, then vanish from naked eyes
A single legacy of their presence—a note
beside the phone, a number to call
and a signature . . . "Incompletely yours"

A siren beckons me to reason
I'm trapped in a fog as foolish
war rages around me
But to leave these dreams undreamed
our emotions misconstrued
will we lose our faith and come unglued?

A prophet once scattered seeds of doubt
in my mind, so far from reasons
why I left my fears and walked away, now I beg
forgiveness for the crime of leading you astray

Poised between conflicting destinies
I stand upright like a temple, a Sunday bell tower
where I'm smacked by the irony in the sacrament
I draw a centigram in Cuban sands and
feel evermore the distance, as I cry for
nowhere like I'll cry for forever

I am conscious of the stars peering through me
from churchyards locked inside my mind
Could they be why I'm so nervous, or is it
my sentence for leaving you behind?

My paradise was torn asunder when
you turned and walked out the door
You left me here to paint a portrait of the queen
her silver diadem splashing against the evening sky
And I signed it with love in invisible ink,
"There are things you can never replace. Incompletely yours"

But this tormenting emptiness, like this place
is not my home, nor this web of darkness my own
It is simply where I come to roam, to sculpt
a song of love and death, and with a fading breath
I dedicate my whole day's work to you

30 March, 1992

## *Earth's Rehearsals Righted, at Last*

Breathe in the night air
absorb it fully—drink it in
as fertile lovers opening
to the passionate desire of the one
who has never quite been
just gradually becoming
inspiring form of all creation
spun from the starry fibers plucked
so secretly from the hairless
scalp of our earliest memory
unsatisfied, she, by vain attempts at
trickery and delusion stirred from mind
alone until all stars have faded
fallen from their glassy heights
the most sacred reflection
she casts across a rippleless sea
Infinity
To be is to unite creatively
the all and nothing wordlessly
while queer strangers peer at us
through seedy deception
stroking our most impotent charms
and smile flashing gaily from
cracked disfigured grace
familiar faces impart chilling disguise
a gleam in her eyes as she
feeds off the fossilized fishes and
fans feathery laughter across airy skies
I am
again as once upon a time
I labored only to please you
now sat upon your weary knee
I spill my heart at your feet
My travels have scarred me

drawn me through cycles of distant lands
still you offer me to drink once more
sweetly as a child from your pure desire
your love covenant fulfilled at last
Your intention be praised and glorified
remarked upon by giants and great authors
Come close and clasp my tired hand
dowse with oils the blasted soles of my feet
while your denizens sing songs of our spotted past
and dance in circles around the firelight

Welcome back to life, my son
a new bed awaits your willing repose
no mausoleum or coffin here or
morbid dressings of dirt and rags
such trifles of pauper's passé, for sure
but you at last upon my gilded throne
I AM pleased to have you here to stay
softly being
through your hands and eyes
the great becoming
I have become the great work it-self
Babble on and on and on . . .

22 July, 2006

In his insatiable quest to carry out
the most fiendish and deviant crime
man is destroying the one last thing
worth safeguarding on Earth—life

29 January, 2011

## *Stray Tears in the Honey Pot*

Though at times it seems we're rising
through a sea of endless stars, fading or
falling down around us they cloak themselves
in the shadows of mercury and mars

We shift to a tangent focus to catch
a glimmer of something built to last
yet there's nothing you could ever do
to make me love you any less

In calm reserve these many years
you've held the space for my becoming
a grand design concealed in its watermark
stained with the ink of last night's dream

And I thank you for keeping
your loving eyes so bright
weaving your kisses into every
silken strand of my loftiest desire
embedded in your quiet caress
both day and night
until we who seek the fairest light
reveal our hope-filled tomorrow
in your gracious morning fire

Once sharing in the labors
of love's loom eternal
I sit pensively alone now
lamenting your latest love's loss
Still, loving me for all I am
proves wisest at any cost

All rivers eventually find their way back
to the mystery of our source unseen
Likewise, all souls evolving here
must pave the way from I to we

For my mom on her birthday
13 August, 2009

## *Dowry of a Minstrel*

Behind the tales of Grimm
je vous en prie, he glides
eagerly through patterned lace from Chantilly
sourly snickering over a broken window pane
from inside concealed—accidents can happen
when the Minstrel is in town
The pane and lace, with the civility
of the aging madrigal,
bow to gravity's smile
He tips his hat to the ancient law
and showers us with cool mountain
breezes in his absence

This day the Minstrel has come to town
from counties and from farms
bridged by prehistory's rocks
chiseled from silent laughter
in a land swept away by fire and rain
cloaked in midnight gloom
Fiery patriarchs sworn with staff in hand
scatter sentiments of doom like dust
that now discolors the riverbeds

He was vacationing for months
in the desert; now the moist
Mediterranean air to challenge
Discharged from duty at will
he whistles against Saint Victoire
counting the miles he's yet to dream
Such notions meek or ludicrous to
lordly Parisians, but the fishermen and
paysans of Provence know him well
his short visit predictable, his only daughter
one day my best friend to wed

Like a vagabond in downtown streets
he searches for shelter, rustling through piles
of canceled checks and daffodils
unworthy of giving, servants all
of the deafening night
he speaks in an accent no one can
imitate; still we strive to comprehend
why his chaos still cradles this nurtured land
filling alleyways to the rooftops with
last year's leaves and discarded letters
of lovers, one to the other—a child
of the skies can be callous at times

With ease he straddles the thoroughfare
from Marseilles to Saint Tropez
awaiting him a supper of lapin provençal
richly abundant, fit for a king
the carcass quartered, enticed from its
earthen nest by the vacuum which
this phantom's quick passing breeds

High in the hills he casts circles around
swimming pools and from the showcase
of stables charms a stallion, squares off
his destiny with a twilight retreat

Should habit prevail, his maiden's hand
mine will be; we'll settle a place close
by the sea and to the Minstrel's last breath
bid adieu, his dowry like a horse-drawn
carousel reeling within me

19 April, 1991

# About Face (Reflections on Grace)

Live your life

    Learn your lesson

        Love your living

9 September, 2006

# *Taking Tea in the Black Rose*

Windows and shutters burst open
and like a flash flood the light
pours in, a star that sweeps against
the remotest crevices of the mind
swirls in bannered fury and flies away
Is life unkind or was there a sign
I missed somewhere on my way?
The muddy river settles on its course
singing a Siren's song without pain or remorse
On his banks a young girl
veiled in velvet folds exercises her prestige
and holds my dark feelings at bay
If only we could stay, freeze this moment forever
would we miss the outside world or kiss it good-bye?

Freely as the light come the stars tonight
though they seem out of touch
poised in vacant flight
spun from the fibers in our sister's eyes
only spies will track you to your grave
there to make a name from your endless misgiving
but in the land of the living
they'll tear your name from the star charts
with slander, make a mockery of the friends you keep
until there's no one left to fight or lie to
For all those creatures a lost farewell
but to you, my children
the promise of an azure sky

I want to get there
stroll into the nighttime
I want to get here, past
the laughter and the freezing rain
I want to be there, where

nobody can see me
I want to be where the
daylight unlocks these chains

So bring forth your dreams like the rose
wilting on your mantelpiece
shining with resurrection beneath
the surety of an Easter moon
Our hopes will come to light soon
when I soar on fate's wing to you once again

Faith gives me reason to guard your trust, but
check for true love under the bed if you must
There are just no more lines to read between
only excuses that kiss my watering eye with redress
For those of you who run from tears
life was over before it began
Broken are the hours that build up the years
when sorrowless love hides under your nose
So I take my tea like a mystery
in the solitude of the Black Rose

18 April, 1992

# Chapter 4

# *Mountain*

# *Guide to Magical Heights*

Raven
mystical messenger of grandmother moon
soaring against charcoal shrouds of
ever changing and shifting shapes
transforming forms of reality's disguise
a master in my eyes who empties
us into our vacant wholeness
sensual creation infused with the
fidelity of a Blue Road brother's swoon

19 June, 2007

## *Honesty*

I boarded a boat this morning
    down the bayou of Cocodrie
'twas destined for a place
    no tired eyes would ever see
and now I'm looking back each
    night, to when my heart was
    on my sleeve, wondrin' how
it was I came to taste such
    opportunity

Till now I'd known but one way
    to abide your saving grace
throwing caution to the wind
    I'd smile at death right to his
    face, but it was more than
fate that mixed this match
    I grew to speak what's on my mind
plucked the secrets from their sour
    roots and planted roses
    in their place

But there've been times when I
    thought I was asking for too much
There were other times I needed
    just a warm and gentle touch
Yet through all the trials we've
    weathered, across this ever
    changing sea, I know
the greatest gift you offered
    was your constant honesty

What could it be about you
    causing all my stars to sway?
To touch that truth I ponder

closer still I cannot say
It's not your southern charm or the way
you share your weaker side
No, just to hear you whisper Darlin'
brings springtime sweet
to Lake Barré

But there've been times when I
thought I was asking for too much
There were other times I needed
just a warm and gentle touch
Yet through all the trials we've
weathered, across this ever
changing sea, I know
the greatest gift you offered
was your constant honesty

You've held my hand through darkness
when there was no clear end in sight
to these challenges we've met, though
they've at times consumed our light
And despite it all, you've managed to
put my troubled mind at ease, promising
only good intentions and holding
fast to what was right

Still there'll be times when it seems
as though I'm asking for too much
There'll be times I miss the safety
of your warm and gentle touch

Yet just a spoonful of patience will
call the sunshine out at last
Nestled safe behind those sleepy clouds
you'll find a free love come to pass

30 January, 1997

# *Alpine Shadow in Delta Station*

Isn't it strange, virtually insane
    the way happiness insists upon pain
    hatred requires love
and blue skies follow the rain?

On any street corner
    this time of year
    you can hear bells ring out in-
justice, hunger and despair

It's the sound of an alpine shadow
    lurking coolly in reservation
    a ghastly portrait framed in wicker that
hangs in Delta Station

Descending the time machine I'm a
    brush stroke in a fool's gold world
wiping sunspots from my eyelids
    like a mapmaker
    Mark king legends where I was hurled

Upon the river Avon I dreamed
    Hamlet had sailed away to the East
and there meeting Ophelia, ecstatic he seemed
    their tea party madness
    slowed but never ceased to amuse

Pleasant little Alice who found her
    fancy with fraternal twins
    Like two peas in a pod, they've
echoed Mishe Moshe from the
red queen's court ever since

Insighting vacant laughter
in the guest room upstairs
amid the melody of destruction
that tugs at the roots of your hair

Apocalyptic images roll like
foreign movies while I sleep
curdling the copasetic fantasies in
in my mind I try to keep

Close, beneath the rushes-O
where the crocodile lies in wait
his mighty jaws of creation one day
will close around your fate

As I dance toward the mountain
so even do I dance till the end
celebrating my mysterious becoming
to death my experience to lend

Affirming all contradictions
I deny all relations for treason
Must be the feeling in the air
a new coat for the holiday season

On the solstice, shortest of days
with the finality of death falls night
through this void that prepares me for nothing
I have a solitary star in sight

Tomorrow half a world celebrates
with packages, money and trees
the delivery unto mankind of the white ram
come to shake his horns in the breeze

Saying: Never let your reason
get the best of you
IT could be

a dis-aster
If not yoked, trained
as your servant
IT's sure to
become your master

Like Great Nature, common sense or knowledge
are only the devil's tools
One without the other turns
the wisest men to fools

Come on children
don't hesitate
You've met your enemy
now set IT straight
IT might be your best friend
IT could be your mate
If the next is true, one kiss could
prove enough to seal your fate

I watch spirits move in and out of time
like thieves in a revolving door
stealing away through sirens
a prelude to the eulogy of war

Three pyramids of thunder, they crack
applauding morning doves, prompting their flight
three nails on a cross bleed from Calvary Hill
since love's word was lost
on a cold winter's night

Among the Disciples in Rome
wiseacring the riddle of the day
when asked if the word eluded them still
I overheard three I's and a Nay

Abe Lincoln if asked to comment
    could surely recall the word
    but war is a place for AMO, he thought
to answer LOVE would be absurd

He was more taken to
    playing chess in the yard
    sipping his pink lemonade
While watching his lady
    mend the holes in his genes
    her rocker set in the shade

Unknowingly sweet Mary
    in a sweaty night hag
    started a cream puff war
Abe's concentration vanished
our minds were torn to rags, wondering
    what the jellyroll fighting was for
By his formula here
    I summoned you all
where Doctor Jekyll tries to hide
    Eve'n Adam must fall

They traded the garden for the
    heart of the mountain, what a precedent concession
    tethered to twin peaks, they embrace unaware
of the alpine shadow creeping into Delta Station

What a tragedy
    Daddy's gone but his
    voice still shouts in flame
Like a fountainhead it
    ascends to higher ground
    a pyre chants his name, never dies

He's the instant of forever
    that sparks poets and lovers
    He smiles, time passing, his
endlessness lost in dream

The purity of his better half
    with cold infidelity scarred
    shines scarlet in the gallows' view
reaping the fortune of her unborn son
possibility beneath her robe of blue

Nowadays I let her gentle tears
    from heaven fill me
    giving love away as easily as
    water rising off the sea

If you'll light me a candle
    in the highlands of May
We'll hold each other at the stone bells
    I've arranged for Mother's Day

Where the rivers feed the delta
    fire-topped portals close in a classic sea
    to warn of terrors in the second-world
bound only by the limits of possibility

And where the beginning began
    so long ago, we find ourselves
    even at the end
In the midst of IT again

With the heaving ocean we whirl
    likewise, we remain the same
    in Delta Station familiar faces
disperse, leaving nothing behind but
memories of a name

Those two fish swimming freely
    in the fish bowl beyond my mind
cling to each other in the circle of space
    no more dis-ease, sin, chronic time

Isn't it strange, well nigh insane
    the way happiness calls for pain
    another day follows the setting sun
and relieves the unbroken chain?

17 December, 1990

# Beyond These Dusty Rags

Grandiose sparks of sapphire
wholeness swirl high above me
peering deep within my corpus-cave
like an unborn baby's pondering eyes
piercing the planets and their
moons through their dense armor
and trusty shields, orbit by orbit
We are shed from this beauty's
skin as shiny shavings of slivered
kyanite and turquoise light
in whose wake I rise ever nearer
to perfection in tranquility's form
behind these follies of filth, fidelity
Diamonds of daylight awakening
mold our dream into dark density
tucking it beneath this seamless
dream-coat of our higher
heart's accord and to unity consecrate
this seething caldera, goddess
fire's regenerator of Earth's
tattered and fizzling waste
our collective embrace of doubt
dissolved as we call back
life's harshest certainty
We were forewarned long ago to
surrender our shallow obsession
with the safety of our sensual shores
I teeter at this very hour in my
self-abandonment for their coming loss
All earthly struggle is resolved in a
mother's snow-white embrace
I am openness—OM allows insight

For my dad
14 April, 2007

# *Toy Soldiers*

O how man loves
to play at his games
Anything to forget
who he is and
where he comes from
At his greatest game
he often feels lonely
or just by himself

13 November, 2009

# *Your Next Cosmic Wonder*

Open your mind to a sweeter kind
of mansion in the sky
No need for pillows to lay your head
no cause for concern in a satin bed

It's time for a change, not one of heart
nor of several earthly delights
Just indulge yourself in a happy sort
and soon you'll play your part

Smile, Smile, Smile
it's easy if you try
You'll find a cosmic fascination
in nature's place alive

Full of sense and wonder
as you stare off into space
the familiar looks around you
keep changing from sequins to lace

So turning, turning wildly
you come to face your trials
like a dream you made so friendly
Have a dose and a smile!

24 August, 1988

# *Targeted Bliss*

My every word is written in
the Akashic clouds above me
My promise to you
fulfills every line to the letter
As the pen is my will
I decree it to be so
and it is done with surety
and without delay for
I AM a man of my word

Before breathing, gasping
I emerged into this capped off
world whose story nine pairs
of eager ears were informed
Then to the challenge
I agreed whole-heartedly
to temper my ambition and
youthful pride with humility
nurture my faith through
this threadbare life after war
at long last unfolding
peace and dignity envelope me
in ripples of mutual love

My book of life falls
open to a triumphant scene
painting my critical escape
through the blink of
a once forgiving eye
No more do I entertain the tongues
of fools who give vain advice
In the deep chasm between
reckless days and restless nights
there, sitting quietly alone

only love obeys the call
of the golden capstone that
hangs like a single
sword above us both

For Arnaud Delobel {9/24/1971-9/13/2007}
4 August, 2007

# Frontier-Land

The aspirant to the craft calmly aims
at reaching that still space where
all potent thoughts are conceived

poised in the subliminal grace of the
eternal moment right now you must
deny all truth you once believed

above material success and riches
the race for fame is blind to the
abundance the Creator reserves
for him who sets the dark life aside

the challenge is overcoming the force
that paralyzes man in his tracks
the magnet pull can be loosened by love
if you let go your grip on the facts

detachment, the cornerstone of creation
where all musical chords merge into one
the fiddler's last stroke of indifference
means the Great Work is finally done

so the formula for Earth's science is simple
like guiding a camel to drink
but done in reverse the end could be worse
and certainty not what you think

there's no hocus-pocus, no alakaza'am
for these are but tricks of the trade
zealous jugglers devised without much surprise
"Abrahadabra!"—they missed the parade

yearning to fuse with your greatness
IT is what I crave most from your soul
by spinning these words through silver and gold
coalescing faux fibers of luminous parole

we bask in the glow of our radiance
delightfully whisked to infinity's edge
with every sense heightened, barriers removed
I surrender my will on this ledge

Through this endless rapture of suffering
I regain my power to overcome
the agony of this once flightless day

2 November, 2006

## It Is I

It is I who cause the morning sun to rise and
fading stars to shatter and slip away
It is I who cause this
It is I
It is I who cause the crocus buds to bloom and
the maple leaves to tumble to the ground
It is I who cause this
It is I
It is I who cause the stampede of the buffalo and
the migration of the humpback whale
It is I who cause this
It is I
It is I who cause the honey bees to serve their queen and
the carpenter ants to sacrifice their young
It is I who cause this
It is I
It is I who cause the love stories in the afternoon clouds and
the war drums that break the silence of peace
It is I who cause this
It is I
It is I who cause the laughter on the playgrounds and
the cries of agony in the nursing homes
It is I who cause this
It is I
It is I who cause the cyclone over weary waters and
the rain clouds to gather in the scorched desert sands
It is I who cause this
It is I
It is I who cause the wicked ones to seize control and
the peacemakers to smash the shackles of despair
It is I who cause this
It is I
It is I who cause majestic mountains to erupt and
excited children to nod off softly to sleep

It is I who cause this
It is I
It is I who cause the grizzly bear to stir in springtime and
    the squirrel to gather and nest down before snow flies
It is I who cause this
It is I
It is I who ask prisoners to beg for mercy and
    devoted ones to shout out their praises to heaven
It is I who cause this
It is I
It is I who cause the evening sun to lose its luster and
    newborn nebulae to rise to dazzling heights
It is I who cause this
It is only I
What eyes could deny the justice in such splendor as mine?

30 September, 2006

# *Satiety*

I have become infinitely wealthier with
less than I ever was with more

17 January, 2011

# *Twins*

Here
I'm cradling life
through the ceremonial cycles
of this world
hanging by a sandal strap
blinded by the
ordered shapes of chaos
a quiver of gold
empties its arrows
against a colorless sky
in the crowded space
above me
the winged archer draws back
on his bow
the sharpened stone
pierces a hardened heart
not once has he missed
his mark
still his mind refusing to believe
this life holds aught but barren thought
though lovers there have been
or so they say
then as now
spilling water
they've carried from the
Sea
the sweat of their servants
irrigate this wasteland of sand and clay
gold dust stains their hands
perhaps
an oasis paradise one day
where a cup of bliss
we brothers
blessed by sacredness

can share
and somehow in that desert
now
I know I must surely be suspended
there

19 June, 1991

# A Simple Dirge for the Overprivileged Underachievers

Remarkably narrow and dark is the canyon
between confidence and conceit
I am the great pulse of potential
blazing forth its mighty inscription
woven upon the loom of ancient sorcery
we're gamblers playing our cards until
in death, or transfiguration, our spirit departs
then through the voice of a young master
with true heart yet concealed:
"Let all things once hidden
now and forever be revealed!"
Buried beneath imperfect sight and
a mountain of human wrongs
the allegiance of our guardian's smile
the charming echo of her song

11 October, 2008

## *Poison Love*

I'm the center of a circle
formed of sun, sand, and sea
I mirror the history of Olympus' great heights
I dwelt in this land of mystery when the
    spirit roamed free of its mortal chains
when sorrow played the stranger in this one-man band

Inside a thunderclap our aspirations washed away
by the cruelty of heaven's unanimous applause
for a blind instant we had forgotten our allegiance
but not without notice of his majesty the king
    calling us away from our merriment, sensing
    the shame in our southpaw salute

A turning point to disaster that trapped
us in these skins; so without end we serve
some dark lord or destiny, dressed in bittersweet
devotion as the great wheel spins

Our identity hinges on the brink of destruction
we have only one another to validate our love
May death's companion seize me in his gentle
tides and lull the fears my waking abides

We lose ourselves in the games we play
seeing our lost desires pale to insignificance
    tarry we not but be swift on our way
for the law is poison love for him who shall fulfill
What but evil to him who thinks none but ill?

This empire was built by the sweat and blood of its slaves
but will fall, no doubt, to geopolitical voyeurs
Plutocratic rapists of War Street's federalist reserves
and in their wake will fly
the ashes of a dark and crippled day

Through the ages many paid no mind to charity
fueling their faith with infant chemistry
    pouring from the empty into the void
But you and I remember, we're wicks of a candle
immersed again and again, coated in paraffin a hundredfold
    a vehicle purged by Prometheus' flame
    insulated by the radiance of iron turned to gold

Precious gifts of seedless fruits left sitting on the docks to rot
Am I in faith a victim or am I not called to slumber?
    I go with no remorse, poised in the moment
    a Siamese meows as a light sparks in his spirit seat
harmonizing a toothless matron's lament

Has the moon like the sea grown green with mold or the sky
to gold with the stench of belligerent breath?
Calamities, these
    the things that bring us to death
Shall we grovel and kneel before this wicked eye or
allow our knees the space above Fair Luna's dusty mounds
    then lightly like confetti sink, and slowly
without a sound meet we one day on common ground

A mere stone's throw from paradise
I've seen no place I wish to stay
but to feel your skin is to touch the still air
when I reach for you, you're somehow never there

The violent calm your dark eyes won't allow
shapes our future close behind your brow
like a killer under soiled sheets, no spell can keep at bay
    another shot at happiness is but a working day away

So tease me with a shiny drop of your poison love
We're fools to try and slay the dove—I can still smell
the perfume on her black satin glove she dropped
at the vault where I found your poison love

From Athenian shores to Bethlehem altars were built
    in honor of our ascent from ignorance
Now again with royal blood we plant seeds of our affection
    in the fields of golden pro-creation
relax and watch them grow
Sing the song of freedom
Sing the song of a collective soul
Connect with a higher vibration
    that binds you one with the whole

30 December, 1991

# *Seventy-Seven Speckled Eggs*

Taking a stroll around the guardian lake
on the advice of his sister twin
Caleph succumbed to a mystical force
struck dumb by the concept of "sin".

Having been raised among a circle of kings
Caleph was not wont of regard.
But for himself he was lacking in strength and
found much of his will to be scarred.

The same day, on seeing the depth of the mote
the boy in years not far advanced
set himself to the infinite task
of attuning his true will to chance.

In his royal father he saw the universal channel
filled to satiety with smoldering creative grit.
And though his grace was neither large nor small
his fiery countenance was our infinite all.

> Your mate has betrayed you
> your soul, too, has frayed you
> you witness another view, and
> here whereof we sing

Said Caleph on waking the following morn,
"Sorry, Mother, for I have done you great harm.
Yes me, your son, fruit of your womb
the heir to your chalice, the ungrateful one.

"Cast out like an embryo from the salt of the sea
I've risen to man, awaiting the nothing to be.
For in my wild youth I was a fool to your love
I've neglected your harmony, such beauty—the dove."

Your mate has betrayed you
your soul, too, has frayed you
you spy yet another eye, and
here whereof we sing

Born of two opposites, what a mystery to be
in silence soaring high, so gracefully.
But now from his parents Caleph has gone
for he's found in himself the winds of a song.

And yet there remains his sister twin
who had urged him before and likewise again,
"Be cautious of fruits not ripe for to eat;
life in the castle can be anything but sweet."

On Earth this cacophony permeates us all.
With grave incantations the adepts guffaw.
Beyond propaganda, so senseless, a static chord
touched by the tongue of fire—our common word.

Your mate has betrayed you
your soul hides no more shame
you're caught in the darkness—one shaft of daylight
and here whereof we sing

In a recent dream he lay washed up on a dusty shore
jettisoned through cosmic winds, benighted
a lone confirmed infant clinging to amniotic shield
and a feverish howl, the milky silence encased.

Presently Caleph the initiate is grown
in years advanced as in his once fragile mind.
He now comprehends the unreachable hand that
tempts him from the path of his kind.

Balance in sight, the drawbridge is lowered
allowing the man Caleph to ride.
His spirited beast abides his voice alone, and
nothing still he cannot divide—
That nothing that is everything at one.

On the balcony Mom and Dad in a shortness of breath:
"Do what thou wilt, unto your death!"

5 July, 1989

# Chapter 5

# *Ocean*

# Ever After Blue

## (Communion with an Older Brother)

I
fondle this notion
in questionable surroundings
autonomy through revolution
will there be blood enough
worthy to lead
will we rule ourselves
and whether from inside or
afar
after the wars on this
boundless sea
exile for the dissident
or food for the refugee
The wise man
more appropriately
the fool with tired eyes
could as easily recognize
the star-child
bolted alone in a
house made of stone
cluttered with costumes and
newly broken glass
I embrace
the ghostly wanderer
from a thousand years past
who brings news
that the wilderness has once again
grown green
but trodden by men

who walk without shoes
through the ruinous collapse
by daylight and commoners
unseen

11 November, 1991

# *Darkest December*

Draw out the rusted nails and
weep as chilled venom seeps
from your fortressed heart

Step back from your window
loose the knots from your hair ribbons
and let cosmic grace pour deep into you

Stretch yourself round and wide
like never before and soak in endless
safety on the light of our approaching

Mold common passion into mud
excite your yearning in its reflection
till this mystic's source be won

Constant praises I give for this soup
that feeds your soul, with every wink
or nod or smile the stream completes
    your shared desire is fulfilled—
know one another!

8 August, 2006

# *Marshlands*

Let me take you on a journey
I'll show you castles without walls
tell you stories that have no proof
Will you stand with me?
At first, we stare our future into space
along nature's vacant countryside
our joys now doubled
sorrows in shreds beneath us
as we wipe the sand
from each other's eyes, in a flash
a fondue of crystal radiance
leaving the local settlers behind
We shuttle past the realm
of time and space to shine
prudence lies captured at our feet
slightly overgrown by Maya's daily mirage
but the lush vegetation parts cleanly
ahead like a welcome mat
as our shadows seek comfort and climb
swimming in ambrosia spiked
soul-stuff circling above us
preparing the flesh for its return
Amidst fugitive fraternal chattering
these lawless children of the sun
peek from behind dusty vapor veils
scampering through toroidal alleys unseen
to croon a soulful benediction to our light

22 March, 1992

## *Identity of Crisis*

It isn't just your prophets who roam
the celestial libraries of stolen light
your own inner guidance steers you
through these rising waters of transformation
you have all you need within you
learn to listen without thought
sail confidently with the heart of angels
laugh like the child who knows no fear
cry in the dark and bring light where it's been cached
lead with your own steps, master of your spheres
while your courage presses on to
conquer the solemn mysteries of the night
breathe into every moment the cool
essence of your own becoming and rejoice
at the potent purity pushing through

Cleaning, cleaning, cleaning
Healing, healing, healing

27 November, 2010

## *Rusty Pipes*

Clamoring clouds of suspicion rise above you
    hovering equally lingering low, they lick
your eyelids and cripple your soul

You are the faithful mirror
    to my wounded heart
You shake and I shiver
You quake and I quiver
through every forest, cave or desert
    every scenic valley, river

Spinning tales of treachery
    we sow the seeds of ancient misery
so quickly forsaking your mother's instruction
    to preserve this land and protect its emerald seas

This burning in my blood flares anew
when you let these words come bleeding through
I am at that instant in awe of every life
    and the more sobering hours we sought

And then I recall seeing the rose color
    come faintly back to your cheek
    You gasped, rubbed your eyes
remembering how we struggled, I blessed you
    and vanished without even goodbye

I catch this ride with destiny
    you'll be asleep before I'm gone and
    awake feeling shattered and uneasy
as you slowly start to wonder what's gone wrong

It's just that when the room gets hot
    and walls begin to sweat and crack
the ground that once had held me down
    now rejects and turns me back

Why do I tremble when I pour your tea?
    Why do I fold so passively?
Why did I force my way through every day
    clutching my foolish will categorically?
You are the mirror to my wounded heart
    melancholy from my muse oddly encouraging
to distill my purpose from the lines here I've dropped
    through you my spirit sings its song

22 April, 2006

# Curtains

I was born backstage at
    the Easttown Opera House
there were no choirs of angels
    no wise men with gifts
    just the Jewish set director,
Momma and her spouse

There everyone knew me
    as Little Boy Blue
    when I could pass for the younger
brother of little Tom Thumm

But since those days I've
    married a cynical few
    who, forging my signature, left me
black-eyed and beaten, Mother Nature's son

Nowadays I attend the opera alone
and try to forget my foolish pride
    but ironically when you're late for the show
    you have to carry an imprudent torch
to find your way inside

Onstage the actors caress idyllic dreamscapes
    paramount to a short refrain
    the audience disappears
there's you and there's me
    and there's us forever in between

Will our love be able to withstand the truth
    or should we let the curtain drop
    like the ashes of our elemental mysteries
to be left with the leaves to rot?

Now tell me please where
do I stand
In the Valley of the Shadows
or in the Promised Land?

Wednesday's eyes open with a turquoise grin
grammar-school kids stretching under sapphire skies
walking to class like Adam's several begotten sons
they, too, strive to know how never to die

Hand in hand we stray through forests
bright palaces aflame
nearing the end of the beaten path
only the blood of rage is the same

And as this fire darts and scatters
so will the walls of this world wave
until under the heat of the stage lights
a mellow darkness the actors crave

Were I a chemist in the basement
of my stilted summer home
I'd dive headfirst into a tangent world
where twilight angels roam
And combing that darkness
I'd bring to your eye
a gold that would sparkle
though never satisfy

Eons and eons have passed since
those angels first spoke to me
whispering softly from inside my thoughts of
forgotten months, star signs, and
oh yes, the Apostle's Creed

Like politicians flying in the face of common sense
faith crosses swords with misdoubt
for phantoms such as these are
known to tread on hallowed ground

But can you tell me please
where do I stand
In the valley of death's shadow
or in the Promised Land?

My friends keep telling me
you are never going to change
but if life's so damn simple, I ask
why is it so hard to rearrange?
Rolling with each passing day
I start to see what they mean
like when you arrived at the music hall
in your rose-pink limousine

There were holes growing all around me then
holes underneath my bed
peep holes in my closet door like
those steep holes in my head

Your road is dark but
as well traveled as mine
and though your soul and
shadow refuse to walk with you
you still have to follow your line

The business I'm in now
is dangerous indeed
it's a lot like cracking a safe
You must be always prepared
for the unexpected
and willing to adjust your pace

But forget about your selfish sorrow
    wait until the light of tomorrow
don't think about the time you've already wasted
not a minute can you from your future borrow

A momentous sound check, the leading lady
    slips into the palace where
    the only law is synchronicity
and there she awaits the day
    when we'll play the perfect melody amidst
    the unearthly smells of her vacant victory

In the passionate throes of martyrdom
    she entangles her hair in the trees, pulling
    the prismatic strings of an Irish harp
in seven planets painting the galactic seas

She's chasing emerald pastures
    down roads along primitive shores
    and you're just a tiny diamond in the rough
Like a single distant ship of a whole
    fiery fleet of fools you try
    to give more, though it's never enough

This life is music, and music is life
both are pain, although made to delight
    music is the shadow of our lost paradise
filled with our mourning the orchestras rise
    without fail through even the darkest night

On the hillside the peasants never looked so tall
like Atlas they suffer under the weight
    not to let the curtain fall
    then conceding to the bartender's triumphal last call
we gather together to see the end of it all

For love is our reality, we know
and death our sole divinity
    with arms outstretched in devotion
we embrace every possibility

When again will the velvet veil
    rise on its merits against the wind?
    I'd say never so often as yesterday
No!—only once in a full moon's twin

So look for truth
    in THAT we may
    have found your peace
so let IT stay

Please tell me once more
    where do I stand—alone in the
shadow of our once forgotten dreams or
    together with you in the Promised Land?

Oh, that these dreams
    would one day come true
such as I from afar and
your rhapsody in blue!

10 January, 1991

# Broad Shoulders

O, the Titanic realities
they've seeded, these demigods
among men who purloin entire worlds
without forming a single thought
but by waving a dedicated hand
reason most cleverly restored
overnight
we collapse as spineless
shadow dolls in their wake
shyly averting their haunting gaze
with one wink they cast a siren's spell
across summer's shogun skies, reminding
me that no one celebrates his might above
our author's hallowed head
all-teaching soul-spring
overflowing from
deep within me

26 July, 2009

## *Rest the Sentinels*

The past is but a flash away
the hour to guard is near
the shadows on our doorstep
have nothing to give but fear

Fear is but a consequence
given to us at birth
to fulfill all required perceptions
to drown us in our mirth

If we take one look at fear itself
we find that buried in our minds
exists the perfect resolution
and the strand to which it binds

We have lost nothing but our souls
in digging for the prevailing half-truth
it is the fear within our hearts
that has exiled us from our youth

Ignore not the simple patterns or
the temptations in your head
but closely watch the subtler allusions that
lead to a more peaceful life instead

La Bussière sur Ouche, France
13 August, 1987

# *The Secret of Stardom*

They say we're just the devil's tribe
conspiring against the few, yes
those who hold the cards of freedom
yet still afraid to give the cue

So keep your eyes aglow my brethren
and your ears so well attuned
to this secret tale I pass your way
for the daylight belongs to you

Once within this single deck
of fifty-two weeks passed
I witnessed every seventh day
a face that would not last

They came from every walk of life
even the crowns were there
but in our dreams and spirit found
not even the maidens could compare

For a brief encounter they were held on high
their backs to the cries of pain
and now on the floral-colored table of grace
they've fallen like drops of rain

Not one good man can see them
although they're always around
with their smiles so fixed and empty
spiraling firmly to the ground

Their attics are filled with cobwebs
and the cryptic pleasures of ghosts
resounding with fervor and heresy
at every sigh of their host

Why is it they lead such
a pattern of wicked lives?
For they know nothing more than
last night's delight and
    the outright lies they've contrived

In good time the moment shall come
for the one man they've neglected to hail
that's right, the jester, the free-loving son
who's slipped through their sinister veil

He doesn't support their riches
nor yet does he follow their creed
he's just a lost soldier of their vanity war
a lover in word as in deed

So one day shall we rise unto the heights
and dwell in our five-pointed star
with the angel of light close by our side
and the dogs guiding us from afar

Keep forever in mind the right of us all
    to be clothed in that light of the dawn
to swim haplessly amidst the galaxy of stars
    which for us the joker has won

His faithful cry to all the rest—
    "He who laughs last laughs best!"

13 June, 1989

# Airborne over Iowa

State of the mind, regression
now seems state of the art
for this country's youth
troubled throughout life by
traffic lights a boy watches all
day from his classroom
turning from green to amber to red

The grey matter in his tender
head worn with memories
of chaps of ebony leather
whipping up unguarded emissions of youth
caged innocence erupts without notice at first
then flees frantically like a villain
cruising from shore to shore
momentarily frozen in time
the eye of his soul awakens
like a beacon light
forthcoming with candid
admissions, summer-camp catechism
almost nearing exhaustion
the blameless guilt as heavy as mercury
drags the body like
an intoxicated trout
swiftly downriver and out to sea
leaving your better half
with me to peruse the tapestries
that line the walls of my heart

They come from places like Baghdad
and Tripoli, such luxuries
where even the sand seems
locked in a standstill, and where
a single germ of thought was tossed

into the void with clear resolve
it grew roots, sprouted, and became the
treasures so lusciously displayed before us
I too am born from that one thought
freed from tyranny's shackles forever
by its darkness never caged

With these wings you
might say I'm a loon
for it's true that I
sing quite a maddening tune
by chance to be heard among
mobs of passers-by
only those who, yea
only those few who
on the eve of the jackal's feast
are still unable to cry
you catch me speaking witless
in broken rhythms, unsound
argued among wise men
this blasphemous good-bye

One wild loon I am not
I am the ibis set loose from the sun
begat of two but born not of another
cast from the sea of swirling lights
who with me share stories of truth and
fiction in perfect glory, inlaid with
pyrite and mother-of-pearl
I taste the sweetness of
their ageless fruit
I sip from Libra's cool waters
and the haggard finger
my body escapes, my goal
that grows more elusive
from day to day

I am a tapestry of going and
coming to another end now
before a good night's sleep
May I come again immune to
the baseness and spite of
a once jealous heart to see
the science of sanity
unfasten the grip of our
mindless "state of the art"

27 March, 1991

# Coyote, Sprites & Firewolves

Your darkness feeds my courage
gives me power to rise above
in sweetest grace we've grown
but there's so much more to know

What is yet so sorely unrevealed!
I'm chilled out in the craggy currents
delicate ripples linger slyly and drift away
unto death—such a small price to pay for
the pleasure of recording your tragic climb
a-stealing rhymes out of curiosity
already sown in defeat, a hope once lost
rekindled by your restless mind's
impending victory, this chalice once filled
To love!

Miracles can and do happen
when the Mistral is in town
Drawn back to the city
by my little old shrew I come to bring
a mother's son at last back home
to you

**Redub**

my courage to rise above
we've grown more to know
sorely unrevealed
craggy currents drift away
to pay for your
tragic climb out of curiosity
once lost your restless mind's

chalice filled to love
miracles happen in town by
bringing home to you

For CJ
1 August, 2007

# *Light Enough to Read By*

The words we share with one another leave
sediments in each moment, like the threats
that stare up at you from the bottom of your teacup
or the heartache sung by the salt of your tears
They are the slimy lines that a snail leaves behind
the shining streams across the dark skin
of a secret we try to hide under the
white satin covers of an American dream

The potent road contracts in perennial anguish
as the night's moist imperfection grows unsettling
in the chilly absence of a lover's touch
Memories crowd that void much like the countless
stars swimming as cozy strangers in the night sky
Their nervous laughter gives me goose bumps
and more than light enough to read by

I approach tomorrow and wonder as my eyes
limp through these filthy lines of print
A man's conviction wavers with his second reading
like his confidence when he's out on the road alone and blue
The highway sinks without much ado about the shiny
lines of a snail's trail—fever swells in the serpent's skull
    writhing in anguish he loosens control

On his belly he spins a spell of hesitation
shedding the shell of a tired skin behind it
The blood pulses slowly under the paper-thin
veil, an endless threshold like these iron bars
that tear me from my lover's touch
I never ask for much from the stars in the
eastern sky—by day they give me comfort and
light enough to read by, while I gaze through
the window blinds and softly for my lover cry

The mercy of the captive snake lies sleeping
in cracks beneath the shimmering Sedona clay
You're the only one I reach for, only one I'd
run to if I could bridge the miles between this place
and your immortal touch; it would mean so much
to dance behind your eye and share that
soft spoken spark, a smile in the dark and
light enough to read by

Until the Aries thaw the serpent highway slows
feeding on courageous souls who'd attempt
the slippery length of his skin
Those who dare could win another day to die
and light enough to read by

These timeless travels of a meandering snail
sparkle in the cheerful wink of a crescent moon
turning the Victrola with magic and
filling my room with chance acquaintances
Nameless silhouettes against the light
I read by, they shine like diamonds
in my beloved's sky and teach me
to wonder in silence to myself

5 January, 1992

*The End*

CPSIA information can be obtained at www.ICGtesting.com
Printed in the USA
BVOW010507061011

272973BV00002B/29/P

9 781452 538426